M000249108

Spectral Realms

No. 14 ‡ Winter 2021

Edited by S. T. Joshi

The spectral realms that thou canst see
With eyes veil'd from the world and me.

H. P. LOVECRAFT, "To a Dreamer"

SPECTRAL REALMS is published twice a year by Hippocampus Press,
P.O. Box 641, New York, NY 10156 (www.hippocampuspress.com).
Cover art: *Puck* by Henry Fuseli, c. 1810–1820.
Cover design by Daniel V. Sauer, dansauerdesign.com
Hippocampus Press logo by Anastasia Damianakos.

ISBN 978-1-61498-322-4   ISSN 2333-4215

Contents

Poems

What If Atlantis . . . ?

Geoffrey Reiter

What if Atlantis sank by slow degrees,
Not overnight, awash in cataclysm?
What if it joined the deep sea's black abysm
Foredoomed first by ten thousand auguries,
Its precious scrolls unread in libraries
By archons spouting speech extolling schism
To incensed throngs anointed by the chrism
Of rage and wat'ry wine in quantities
Too full for any mortal mind to bear?
What if its minor prophets' imprecations
Crashed lifeless on the armor of their pride,
Eyes lusty, glassy, glossy, unaware
That each night's sticky, sickly sweet libations
Blot out th'encroaching taste of saline tide?

Painting the Pandemic

Ian Futter

Pus yellows
and the gangrenous greens,
putrescent pinks, which churn between
the bloodless browns
and cancer blacks
from liquid lungs
and tumour stacks.

The bilious blues
and rotting reds
make purple pustules
of our dread,
and forces fellowship to fade
in rancid rainbows,
nature made.

With lockdown legions
welding fast
our dungeon homes;
once castles, past,
where sickly sirens,
singing shrill,
shriek out
the numbered dead and ill.

So sinks the devil
in this slime,
wherein he dances
to my rhyme;
And brings to blister,
with each grin,
a cankered chaos
to our kin.

And while we wheeze
in death machines
we dream of what
we might have been,
and gulp delusions
with each gasp
from futures that
we will not grasp.

Safe

Christina Sng

If I could seal the entrances
Of my home with blood,
I would gladly open
Every artery of mine
To keep my children safe
From the demons outside.

But now, all I have
Are locks and levers,
Easy broken by brute force,
So I reinforce the entrances
With what I have—
The rage of my sisters

Who have died before me,
Our single voice
Louder than banshees,
Our rallying cry sealed
In a motion sensor device,
Ready to be released

When they try to break through
The doorways of my home.
That night, I hear their screams

And see their splattered sinews
Decorating the outside
Of my bedroom window

When their bodies exploded
From the resonances
Of our ultrasonic cry,
Calibrated to the rhythm
Of their movements.
Tomorrow again, they will try—

And tomorrow, I will be waiting.

In the Black Hours

Ann K. Schwader

The gold goes first, each fine & shining prayer
recast as dust. To dust we must return,
however glittering in our despair
against the dark & all we never learned.

Recast as dust, to dust we must return,
despite the silver sibilance of saints
against the dark. And all we never learned,
released at last from parchment's restraint

(despite the silver sibilance of saints)
spawns lurkers in the margins. Snarls of vine
released at last from parchment's restraint
ensnare alike the damned & the divine

turned lurkers in the margins. Snarls of vine
obscure these tarnished platitudes which once
ensnared alike the damned & the divine
with promises of paradise. Affronts

obscure & tarnished, platitudes which once
poured out like wine . . . all fade together, laced
with promises of paradise. Affronts
forgotten, now. Each holy scene erased,

poured out like wine. All fades together, laced
with iron gall night in memory of one
forgotten now. Each holy scene erased
might be some office of the dead begun

by iron gall night in memory of one
obliterated. As each fragile page
might be some office of the dead begun
too late, the book itself betrays its age,

obliterated page by fragile page
till only dark remains. Unmade by grief,
too late the book itself betrays its age
as shadowed dust once brilliant with belief,

now only dark remains. Unmade by grief,
however glittering in our despair—
that shadowed dust once brilliant with belief—
the gold goes first, each fine & shining prayer.

—After the *Morgan Black Hours*, MS M.493

The Woses

(a long-line ballad)

Frank Coffman

There dwells within Old England's forests deep
A breed of fell and fierce wild, hairy men;
The few and dwindling numbers of a race
Once far more common, now but rarely seen.

This feral terror towers o'er the tallest men
When his full, fearsome growth the fiend does gain.
And there are legends that strong knights have sought
To test them in combat—only to be slain.

They are the Woses—Wildmen of the Wood—
With matted hair and fearsome eyes of flame.
They wield as weapons heavy wooden clubs,
And none are sure exactly whence they came.

But folk who live near Albion's sylvan bounds
Still warn their children not to wander in.
"The Woodwose lurks in there; you'd best beware!
For many who dared have not been seen again!

"Even their womenfolk and wild offspring
Would be beyond your scant strength to defeat.
Their cruel, sharp teeth and rending claws would rip
Your poor, young life away. It's Death you'll meet."

So, Traveler, if you think them only tales,
That those wild ones are just the stuff of story,
I tell you I've come upon full many scenes
Of smashed skulls and the ground all grim and gory.

And you'd do well to heed this sage advice:
Especially at night, don't dare to walk the Wood,
For they still lurk among the shadows deep,
And the price you pay may well be paid in blood!

The Man with One Head

Lori R. Lopez

They dubbed him a freak, a circus reject.
He might be a nice fellow, the type to respect,
if they could only overlook his glaring flaw—
plainer than the nose or the cut of his jaw
on a visage that wasn't exactly wrong . . .
No aspect he possessed did not belong.

In adding up virtues, there was much to subtract.
A dozen fingers couldn't count what he lacked.
The list would be long of tallying crosses,
of tipping the scales to weigh Albatrosses.
It was widely known a pair of heads beat one,
and less than two-faced was superior to none.

Losing his noggin he would have none to spare!
Lending an ear in a show that he cared,
what he heard would be slanted, all the same sided.
No balance or logic. Severely divided.
So tragic a figure seemed best to ignore—
a man with one head, a wretch to the core!

Misshapen, a defect, abandoned by his mother?
No kindred embrace. Unlike any other.
A walking weirdo, the man with one head

was impossible to accept, an object of dread
who frightened small kids and the elderly
from his state of single-minded abominy.

I wished I could salvage this hopeless case
beyond the hands of a Surgeon to replace
an absent gourd, those missing features;
a poor self-image, the strangest of creatures.
I pitied the outcast, what he had to endure:
the suffering and hatred, a lifetime impure.

In a world where perfection ranked too high,
the man with one head was no regular guy.
His abnormal traits were innate to detest,
like elevating paleness above the rest.
A Color Scale served to determine worth,
a Waistline Tool for measuring girth.

Blanching and Dieting topped the charts
on a globe obsessed with Appearance Arts.
The lowest of the low were in their own class,
yet high-level citizens did not get a pass.
You could fail any day to live up to codes.
The Scores diminished as a cliffside erodes.

Existing by numbers meant yours may be up!
The man with one head held an empty cup
since the Novelty Shoppe closed, out on the street;
begging for kindness, for something to eat.
I could not risk detection or coming up short,
disregarding him daily to avoid a Report . . .

My noses averted in case of bad smell.

Sensing he smiled and would wish me well.

H.P.L.: R.I.P.

Manuel Arenas

Beyond the Wall of Sleep, in atramentous bardo
Shuddersome scenes replay, ever in eldritch tableau.
May Eve at Meadow Hill, cultists chant their baleful song
"Iä! Shub-Niggurath! Black Goat with a Thousand Young!"
Innsmouth maids, lain with frogs, breed an amphibian race
Hominine until time shows their Demi-Deep-One face.
Richard Upton Pickman, with aberrant ghoulish flair,
Paints his nightmare visions ensconced in his North End lair.
At the dark libraries of the Miskatonic U.
The *Necronomicon*, grave, is laid away from view.
In dim, sunken R'lyeh, the Great Old Ones dissemble:
Constrained Cthulhu bides to surge as dreamers tremble
Whilst direful Outer Gods in unlit space are scheming.
In his grave at Swan Point, dead E'ch Pi-El waits dreaming.

The Appeals of Arianwen, Recruiter of Monsters

A Celtic Nursery Rhyme

Carl E. Reed

Historical note: In 60–61 C.E. Queen Boudicca led the Iceni tribe in a revolt against occupying Roman forces. Following her husband's death, the independent Celtic kingdom of East Anglia (roughly a little larger than modern Norfolk) was wrested from her and previous donations to influential Britons confiscated. Seneca increased this pressure by demanding immediate repayment in full of all loans forced upon the tribe and its allies. When Boudicca protested these tyrannical actions, she was flogged and her daughters raped. The outraged queen (described in primary sources as a statuesque woman with a mane of "the reddest" hair falling below her waist, a piercing glare and a ringing voice of command) took the field against the legions. . . .

Mossman, Mossman—have you any fish?
Bring them home to mother in a bright silver dish.
Rock troll, rock troll—have you any gold?
Pay our gallant fighters: strong, brave & bold.

White Lady, White Lady—hear our groaning moans;
the burning fields are fructified with blood & broken bones.
Dormarch, dormarch—hound of mountaintop,
hurry to Camulodunum—our beloved queen was flogged!

Red fairy, blue fairy—who stomped your nests?
The legionnaires of Nero: loathsome Latin pests!
Wolf thing, wolf thing—have you any meat?
Fast-lope to Londinium: sweetmeats to eat!

Green goblin, green goblin—break out vile poisons.
Dip your arrows deep in tar foul, fierce & noisome!
Black dragon, black dragon—the time is truly dire;
hie to Verulamium: set Roman flesh afire!

Under a Sun Long-Estranged

Scott J. Couturier

Under a sun long-estranged—
corpse-pale skin steaming,
eyelids seared away,
fangs crumbling to ashen cones.
Nosferatu—night's avatar—
sibilant bloodsucker of
centuried, weary age.

Under a sun long-estranged—
blinding white virtue
imbued with life's richness,
succor only when bound
to blood: now, an acid bath
bright & terrible, ecstatic
agony wed to awe.

Under a sun long-estranged—
orb dreaded & loathsome,
cursed oft with vile crypt-oaths
as it crept forth to feed. Now—
a gasp floods grave-withered
lungs, hands fiercely taloned
decaying to swift dust.

An immortal unmade—
once lord of inimitable
under-realms, crowned in

tangled rat-kings, squirming
tails tortuously entwined.
Each night glut on virgin's
effluence, parasite in rut.

Now, oblivion its enterprise.
Too long lurking in tombs,
rifling amid mummia
in mimic of the worm:
light, once abhorred, sole
remedy to its undead state.
A cry as irisless eyes dissolve.

Yet—what luster they
behold before liquefaction!
A moment of near-mortal joy,
coupled to torment unknowable:
pangs as its pea-sized heart
bursts into purifying flame—
under a sun long-estranged.

The Wicker King's Palace

Maxwell I. Gold

In a great hall built of twigs, rattan, and stone, I smelled the natural odors of incense and flame lingering in the air. I was certain I finally found refuge, where through the rotted trees bodies of decaying birch and floundering willows littered the browning forest floor. Past the bony arms of sad wooden ents, I saw the burning wicker palace. No one knew or could have guessed how long the flames had been festering under the pale glint of a dying moon. Long enough it had been, for the stars to lose their lustre as they glared down at the old king's ruin.

The thorny gates of pine and oak, riddled with termites, horrid sprites, and other perfidious creatures crumbled and fell to instant doom as the old hinges squealed, giving me free rein to enter the wicker king's poor domain. Plumes of black, grays, and silver created a voluptuous ceiling of rolling smoke and ash high above me, stretching down every corridor and staining each pillar. My lungs soon became clogged with an unbearable feeling, as if some nameless thing had poured an unholy broth of toxic phlegm down my throat luring me into a terrible coughing fit. The sound echoed down the rambling hallways, only that once it returned the voice was not mine. Some retched filthy scratching flew back at me with a cry unimaginable in this reality.

The mucus settled in my lungs, my voice reaching for words, but silence throttled my attempt. In the crack and calm of the billowing smoke above, I heard it again. Somewhat audible this time, but the guttural thrashing came again; through the singed arches followed by unmatched footsteps. The smoke soon became thicker, heavier, and my body felt liquid, as if something was flooding my senses with a dark sinister opiate. Figures turned to shadow, and smoke seemed like something visceral, material, and tangible. The coughing returned; down the corridors I heard the vile noises boil up to my ears, only this time there was a man not even a man, but some ancient thing skulking down toward me. Belching and coughing the ashes and dust of a thousand dead generations, the Old King's fire was going out.

The Runic Sword

Fred Phillips and Leigh Blackmore

In times forgotten, wealth ill-gotten grew by blades so bold.
In bygone days, in cold winds' haze, when few lived to grow old—
'Twas then was found upon the ground a blade of strange design.
What was its history? Deep the mystery; wise men racked their minds.

This runic sword—whence had it come? From cultures long ago?
What steady hands on savage strands with force and fire and blow
Had fashioned it, as from Hell's pit, in days of fear and pain?
What fallen dust since ere it thrust 'neath snow and heat and rain?

Its pommel carved, its metal starved for blood of fallen foe,
On souls it gorged when first 'twas forged in aeons long ago.
Its blade with runes of suns and moons, rust-black with age and time,
Still hard and deadly, through the medley—sun and sleet and rime.

Not every man, you understand, of mettle strong and free
In very sooth can grasp the truthful price of liberty;
And in a word, not every sword, in fire cast and clear
As tales could tell, will serve so well the folk residing here.

The sword-of-runes brought many boons; it served us well in war,
Unholy blade that with us stayed and slew; with blood and gore
It made its mark, the lesson stark—beware that fateful blade
From out the past or else, aghast, your lifeblood's toll be paid.

The looters came, well earned their name; they burned, they stole, they slew.
Our folk they wasted, mounted, hasted; succour straitly flew.
Now late o' night, by firelight, our kin the fable hear,
Reck not how long to sing this song, yet further villains fear.

List well our rede and keenly heed the moral of our tale,
Lest morrow sing of churl or king with woes anew to wail,
Put not thy faith in ghost or wraith, whatever arms they bear,
But till thy field and let it yield the fruit ye nurture there.

Place little faith in ghost or wraith, no succour haunts their trail.
But hone the blade thy father made, that peace it may avail.

Caged Animals

Steven Withrow

The girl I was was a timid mouse
When we came to stay at the summer house
    Of Crazy Jane, my mother's friend.
    (She earned that nickname, in the end.)
She had no children, nor a spouse;

She seemed to be from a grander age
Of passenger ships, or the opera stage;
    Wore dressing gowns and her hair pinned up;
    She served me tea in a china cup;
And she kept a cockatoo in a cage.

The white-bodied bird had a yellow crest,
A curved black bill. And as a guest,
    Though shy of Jane, I could approach
    That imposing cage and quietly coach
Him to mimic a phrase: *You love me best.*

I fed him grapes as we worked on words;
He wasn't among the most brilliant birds,
    But we practiced for hours. Then Jane swept in
    While Mom was resting: "You won't be kin
To creatures till you've joined their herds

Or flocks; have dwelt in the fox's den
Or the honeybee's box." And when
    I tried to ask her how she knew
    So much about the cockatoo,
She signed the air, in feather pen,

And thus transformed me. Here I perch,
The white bird's mate. I've ceased my search
    For methods of escape. She turned
    Mom to a toad, and I have learned
To be stone, like a gargoyle on a church.

Jane visits us less frequently,
But she adds to her menagerie
    Each time she does. There's now a crow
    Who used to be a man, and a doe
With a woman's eyes. And I can see

My mate was once a human boy.
We cannot speak, but still enjoy
    The silences. (Mom died last year.)
    Strangely, there's an egg, I fear,
To save from Jane, I must destroy.

Odysseus May Have Been a Scoundrel

Darrell Schweitzer

Yes, Odysseus may have been a scoundrel,
a reckless captain who loaded himself down with loot,
raided innocent towns on the way home,
beguiled a witch, blinded the Cyclops,
braved Scylla and Charybdis
(taking a few casualties during each adventure),
until he had lost the entirety of
ships, crew, and treasure,
only to arrive in Ithaca a ragged wastrel
and sow a harvest of death.
By contrast,
Aeneas was a paragon of every virtue,
who carried his father on his back
out of the flames of Troy,
spurned the Carthaginian queen
when duty and destiny called him,
conquered foes and sired such progeny
as would one day rule
all the fairest parts of the world.
But which one seems vivid, a real man,
rather than a shadow,
alive, rather than a mere exemplar?
It isn't the unblemished hero.

I think the gods (not to mention the poets)
prefer tragedy, with a sprinkling of rascality
added for spice.
Suffering holds attention in a way
the exaltation of victory seldom does,
if only because we all have suffered,
we all have fallen short of our ideals,
and very few have ever been truly victorious.
If the end of life is the ending of life,
if even Rome, serene and glorious,
must wait for the barbarians,
then our only recompense is among the shades,
in the cold dust,
where all men are equal.

The Widow

Ngo Binh Anh Khoa

A spider crawled inside her ear
When she was fast asleep
And ate its way into her brain
Where it would burrow deep.

It'd slowly eat the cells it crossed
To build a nest within,
Replacing neural pathways with
Its silky threads therein.

When she awoke the following day,
A weirdness she'd catch on;
As soon as such a thought came, though,
It was suppressed and gone.

She'd go about her daily life,
Oblivious of the change;
Her body functioned normally;
Nothing as yet was strange.

She'd spend time with her doting spouse
And go to work each day;
She'd do her job; she'd share her chores;
She'd eat, and sleep, and play.

The subtle signs, though, soon began
With spells of brief migraine,
Which fast grew in severity
And caused her constant pain.

And yet, as if some inner voice
Had banished the idea,
She would not ask for outside help
Though help was always near.

The torturous days just forward flew
Until one fateful night,
When full control the spider took;
She could do naught to fight.

The mutant thing had grown in size
And had replaced her brain;
Thus, what the creature so desired,
She'd be compelled to gain.

It pulled its puppet to the wild
To catch a worthy mate,
Which crept its way inside her skull,
Where they would copulate.

The pheromone from long-spun web,
Like Ariadne's thread,
Would guide the male through the labyrinth,
And to the prize ahead.

As for the senseless doll in flesh,
She, too, by lust was moved;
Unconscious steps led her towards
Where she'd be worshipped, loved.

Aggressive and without restraint,
Her hips moved rapidly
To drown both her and her beloved
In depths of ecstasy.

And faster, fiercer, harder till
The sought release was reached;
She kissed his nose, and lips, and throat,
Where sharp teeth through flesh breached.

His throat was ripped apart right then,
And death came instantly;
The Widow kept on feasting still;
Insatiable was she.

Once satisfied, she sighed and stood,
Her face and bosom red;
Thin fingers on her belly skimmed
As she got off the bed.

The Widow staggered out of there
And sat down in her room;
Her mind then conjured thoughts of eggs,
From which new life would bloom.

The more she dreamed, the hungrier
The creature would grow then,
So she'd head to her husband's room
And start to eat again.

The spider crawled out from her mouth
To claim its rightful share,
And, having formed a taste for flesh,
It crept back to its lair.

The lady and the spider would
Feast on the corpse each day
For three whole days ahead until
The food dwindled away.

By predatory urges moved,
She mobilized once more;
She washed herself and got dressed up,
Then headed towards the door.

More thoughts of eggs and prey appeared
Inside her hungry mind
As she walked out the house and roamed;
More fresh meat she would find.

She lured more men back to her nest,
And had her way with them
Before a bite, precise and swift,
Left them forever numb.

She dropped down near a mangled form
To let her mind roam free
And thought of nothing where she sat,
Eyes staring vacantly.

The spider meanwhile dreamed of nests
For its expected kin,
New skulls for them to burrow deep
And cast their webs within.

Man of Gold

DJ Tyrer

The savants built God
A great, tall man of gold
Powered by steam and a flame
That burns intensely cold
To govern and to guide
To groom the human race
A thing of terror
With a beautiful face
Enthroned it rules
With a benevolent eye
But when it stands
Its worshippers begin to die
Out into the world it strides
Exhaling a chill breath
That touches those who worship it
Spreading icy death
Until all the world is dead
And it's left without a friend
Alone in an empty world
Alone until the end

The Plague Maiden's Footprints

Claire Smith

We're all swallowed by a black cloud,
like swarms of locusts, a plague eats its way
across the world. Our organs invaded: liver,

kidneys, lungs. They take it in turns
to shiver the story of a hag, poisoned
apple, and a sleeping princess over

milk-sour tea and stale lumps of bread.
Piles of dirty dishes, and saucepans,
spoons, forks and knives stand to attention

ready to attack me. Laundry blockades
the bathroom; while the fireplace
is besieged by dirt, ash, and cinders.

I'm taken to where she rests in a glass
mausoleum, crafted from crystals
they mined. He unlocks the gate,

before leaving me. I creep in; I wind
chains through the door-handles;
I snap a padlock shut so we're locked

inside—my lips are ripe for the kiss.
She's laid on top of a plinth. I climb
up to her velvet coffin: her eyelids still;

a facemask covers her nose, mouth, chin;
her gown is creaseless, white. I lean
into her face, feel her warm breath

against my cheek. I shield her in my arms;
protect us from the diseases' blackened
spread. I look up, know together

we'll see the cosmos, safe, through
the roof of rainbow skylights . . .

A Miscreation of Life

Clay F. Johnson

Deep within the blackest fathoms
Of the frozen star—*the dead star*—
Lives something frozen and lifeless,
Born from nothing it exists deathless

Its shadowless features capture
The qualities of endless time,
Reflecting silvered mirror-shards
Of unimagined centuries

> *Although no water ever existed*
> *The creeping ice grows mangled and twisted*

The star was born a pale blue
Hyper-giant, ignited with sapphire-
Flames for several eternities,
Until it burned opal-white for
Several more, turning to vivid gold,
Rustic amber, then scarlet red
With exquisite flames of liquid ruby

As the blood-red glow faded, it turned
Deathly-cold—*a dying black-dwarf*—
And dimly faint in the lifeless black,
Until at last it succumbed to darkness,
Falling into everlasting shadow

Within the creeping shadow
Passes a lifeless eternity—
Nebula clouds of gossamer'd
Spectral-greens gives birth to stars,
Burning for thousands of cosmic years,
Until the singularity
Of the *black-dwarf* fades and slow-dies
To something occult and unknown:
Ancient star-lore calls it a *shadow-dwarf*

A thousand new galaxies formed
While the *shadow-dwarf* sat silent,
Misremembered, and lifeless cold—
Even its former light—fifty-
Thousand light-years away—extinguished
And exists no more in the endless dark

    Within the depths of its coldest shadows
    An ice-crystal'd orb takes a living form and grows

Growing, yet unalive, frozen
On a forgotten star no longer
Glowing, the living ice exists
Unaware of the shadows of time,
Unaware to the awakening light

Knowing no ghosts
Or creatures of night,
The creeping ice grows alone
Within the coldest shadows,
Ageless—deathless—and full of miscreated life.

Two Haiku

Harris Coverley

Sprite

lithe like waterfalls
more solid than a shadow
hanging on the wind

Bleak Eden

the wilting blossom
man but a passing fancy
flowers for the Earth

In Vino Veritas

David C. Kopaska-Merkel

Under the standing stones there are holes,
inside the holes, boxes,
below certain boxes,
stairs lead down.
Ghouls live there,
and also dholes,
about which the less said, the better,
but the mushroom farms stretch for miles.
The ghouls don't tend the fields;
the dholes are, of course, dholes.

My Aunt Ellen,
if you can believe it,
harvests the mushrooms,
she who once lived
down the street from me;
Uncle Henry processes them,
black smoke pours from the shed out back,
day and night,
though of course,
here there is no day.
The ghouls dislike the smoke,
they rarely trouble the fungal farmers.

When the mushroom wine has done its time,
ghouls cluster thickly,

buzzing like flies at rotten meat,
of course they don't buzz,
and all the meat is rotten;
they scatter like roaches if the dholes come.

That peculiar wine never makes it up here,
you may find empties
lying near fresh stones,
there may be residue in them;
leave it be,
unless for some reason
you need the services of a ghoul.
This vintage is strictly for the post-interred.
Look alive if the ghouls do come;
move faster than your portly friend,
and I shouldn't have to tell you this again:
beware the dholes.

The Chants of Moros

Wade German

On a cliff overlooking the Gulf of Sorrow, the taunter, wearing only an old rope wound about his withered and sun-beaten body, begins to croon awfully, and then to howl balefully, at those who struggle in the water below, singing to each in turn: "Your eyes echo the pungent colour of realization, fixed in that alien mask which is, in fact, your very own image! Listen: all things are inchoate, having ceased to hold any form of charm or enchantment for you.—See! Black clouds sweep across the cerulean slate of the sea. What? The black clouds are merely metaphors for your thoughts and dreams? Ha!—The ocean beneath you is deep. Down below, the octopus of bitter disappointment is already eating your corpse! O, octopus! Leave a few snails for my pot!—Rejoice! The wings of despair flap and flutter around you; the slender lamia slithers from her grotto to lick the contagion-rich, crimson jelly sweating from your incredulous brow. O void of Hope, utterer of reptilian lies!—Hey, you there! What, still clinging to the ledge? Only leap! The precipice despises your touch.—Let my song inspire the breath of the beyond within you.—I congratulate you and offer my condolences at once, seeing Horror become harmonious with your mind! How insipid are your woefuller woes, your dooms undone by incredible dooms!"

Those Who Rise from Orange Slime

K. A. Opperman

We rise from out the orange slime
Of pumpkin guts and stringy seed;
We come at the appointed time,
The night of Halloween to heed.

We do not live, but cannot die
Until our purpose is complete.
Beneath the late October sky,
We shamble down the lamplit street.

Each autumn squash you cruelly smash
Becomes our carved, half crumpled face;
To snuff the jack-o'-lantern's flash
Ere midnight speeds our creeping pace.

All those who carelessly transgress
Against the rites of Halloween
Will know our cold and wet caress,
And nevermore again be seen.

Dionysus in San Rafael

Thomas Goff

> Now, with the earth for board,
> The bread is eaten and the wine is poured . . .
> > —Clark Ashton Smith, "The Hill of Dionysus"

Lines from the Necromancer's late resurgence,
Named for a small mount of pleasure if not vices
In San Rafael. These picnickers, no virgins,
Filled with restored spring energies, are three:
Smith; poet Eric Barker; Madelynne Greene,
The dancer, stretch their lungs luxuriously,
Have labored with their legs to a serene
Where—likely star-point capping this triangle—
Madelynne, dress flung to grass, now leaping nude,
Feels air and light and motion gently wrangle
For sway in sculpting, contouring her. Rude
With health (remember *sur l'herbe*, the *Dejeuner?*),
Clark and Eric cavort about their priestess,
Till wine and food have drugged these men of Manet
Just shy of transmuting ecstasy to a tristesse.
All dizzy, ring-around-the-rosy prone,
Sandwiching voluptuousness and calm . . .
Between their camel's-hair shoulders both men groan
Contentment, from their pavane, from the balsam
Of breeze, odd incantations in their heads.
Three in a heap, the suited, the nude, entwined.
And how is it with her, being the broken breads

Shared out between them, or the freshly vined,
Pressed and fermented drink to be imbibed,
Reconstituted loaf and liquor delicious,
To re-split, consume, her carnal form inscribed
On bacchanalian parchment, vestal, salacious?

Sisters

Chelsea Arrington

Sister, O sister, the time has come
To square scores old and new.
Come now, my dear, do not be glum.
Drink from my acrid brew.

Hearken my song, a lullaby.
Don't sleep until it's done.
Seek my soul, eye to eye:
Behold the blackened sun.

As I spin upon my wheel
So too your mind will whirl.
Dagger to breast is what you'll feel
You vile, repugnant girl.

Eyes once blue now dull as slate
Begin to turn to cloth.
Tears won't flow, you've sealed your fate.
Your hubris pledged your troth.

Out your mouth, do ashes float.
You shall not speak again.
Ever clenched, your pale throat
Will only cry in vain.

Sister, sweet sister, my song is done.
No more my voice you'll hear.
You are lost, my battle won.
Farewell, my sister dear.

An Ill Wind

David Barker

Wash your hands and you'll be fine;
in the flesh the demons dine.

Do not touch your mouth or eyes;
that is where the danger lies.

Keep your distance to survive;
crowds help devils spread and thrive.

Shun all others; stay away—
meeting lets the furies play.

Do not breathe the tainted air;
vapors kill without a care.

Keep your distance; don't draw near—
with each gasp inhaling fear.

Every touch and every breath
can bring sickness, even death.

Sirens wail throughout the day—
haul the dying ones away.

Sunset's when I'm gripped by fright;
death marauding in the night.

But the evening's deadly still;
fiends unseen rampage and kill.

Poison, poison in the air,
slaying people everywhere.

Shadow and Fire

David Schembri

She emerged from dark, from loss, from grief,
Nurtured was the soul of disbelief,
In seclusion, brewing hate is chief,
From the dark, she scales her massif.

'Neath the moon all folk are full of cries,
From a shadow where foul death applies,
Cutting victims under the black skies,
Is the creature of no compromise.

Terror surges out in vein-like streams,
Soaring now, she tries to aid their screams,
Tangled in the Shadow's dreadful dreams,
Beaten down and agony now teems.

Prisoned deep within a woeful vale,
Hanging, crucified by rusted nail,
Ripping free and burning down her jail,
Tortured soul now cracks her vengeful tail.

Blackness grows and runs the rivers red,
Shattered people sink with fears of dread,
Cowering until their hopes are dead,
Shadow grins, its misery is spread.

Thunder rumbles 'neath as clouds make room,
Shadow hunts with anger in full fume,
Rain of fire as she returns in bloom!
From the brink she seeks the monster's doom.

Clashing hard as shadow now meets light,
Hopeful people stand and watch the fight,
Furious, she toils to break the blight,
Killing darkness with her fiery might.

Brighter skies as inky waters clear,
Folk now gather round her; free of fear,
She now dies; they fall and shed a tear,
Years to come, they'll praise her deed with cheer.

Jack Bloodybones

Adam Bolivar

A boggart stalks the moor at night
    And haunts the altar stones;
I pray you never catch a sight
    Of Old Jack Bloodybones—

Some say he's lived a thousand years;
    Some say ten thousand more;
He lurks in dreams and darkest fears,
    His hands stained red with gore.

What quickens him cannot be known,
    Nor why he hungers so,
His body but a bag of bones,
    Which cast a phantom glow.

When from their homes do children stray
    Like sheep into the heath,
Upon them starving Jack will prey,
    And tear them with his teeth.

There was a witch called Betty Crow
    Who learned to conjure Jack;
She carved a stack of runes to throw
    And kept them in a sack.

She sent her puppet to torment
    One who her love had spurned,
And soon from him his limbs were rent,
    A lesson cruelly learned.

Then came the day she got her due:
    Jack trapped her in a dream;
Her bones across the moor he strew,
    Her blood a scarlet stream.

The Arms of Death

G. O. Clark

Is it the voices
of sirens or angels we hear
out there in the fog;

death upon the
rocks, or the warm embraces
of heavenly creatures;

their voices beckoning,
do we dare draw any nearer,
ignore our compass,

lower our sails, the
coin suspended in mid-toss
above the tiller?

Their hypnotic songs
are legend, tendrils of melody
tugging at our souls,

the last thing we know
before our ship explodes into
splinters upon the rocks.

The songs of angels
are hymns of welcome to
the ethereal realm,

the siren's deadly tunes,
the flipside of the same record;
arms of death waiting.

Nightmares of Ink, Dreams in Blood

Maxwell I. Gold

Far off in some polluted dreamland, where the skies were painted with copious amounts of blood and bile, silver-winged wraiths scratched against the vaulted ceilings of night. I watched their clawed appendages dance with sinister jubilation, black ink dripping from their yellowed teeth while I cowered under the streets. No one knew what they were, or what kind of unreasonable furies had wrought such a cataclysm, bringing these horrid beings into our reality. With voices so awful, the howling murderous cackles slithered through my eardrums, strangling my neurons with a sensuous delirium.

Below, I waited, under the ruins of a dying city, my body drenched in the sewage and muck of a lost generation. Time had become mythology; the only measurements of my prolonged confinement were the scratches, feedings, and the endless waiting. The scent of rust permeated my nostrils, rousing me from my dreamy stupor, only to feel the dusty covers of asphalt tremble from above. I knew they would find me, as I saw the dripping light of silver and crimson pour through the crackling holes in the broken streets, as the ink began to pour in through. Laughter followed, so horrendous, mired by the sounds of thick bubbles popping, churning, and stewing, as they hungered for what was left of me. The pounding of hooved feet grew noisier, more urgent as they put more pressure on the concrete sky above my head.

Ink soon poured through the holes, pieces of metal, wires, and grime falling like some putrid snow. Those monstrous voices grew louder, stamping their feet against the dead earth, each thump louder than the last, causing my spine to rupture. The last bits of light were soon blotted out, followed by wild screams, the manic flapping of leathery wings clogging my senses mixed with an overture of unnatural cosmic bedlam.

The immensity of nothingness crowned the living blackness that swallowed the light around me, whispers from the void that once were stars caressed my face. At least, I think it was my face. Sounds of liquid particles, droplets of some kind pierced the calming dark as if I could feel my own consciousness beating against the fabric-web of stars, floating helplessly, without any control. No monsters, no winged wraiths; it was as if I had become a droplet, falling without purpose in this bleak schism of cyber-blackness; this dreamscape of swampy living ink.

Dripping with the ink and blood, inside a cracked vault, waiting for the inevitable, I sloshed at the bottom of night curdling under a leathery flapping, and the smattering of ancient teeth; hanging without purpose, dangling without reason.

The Dominion of the Wicked

Jordan Zuniga

Fire breathes, sulfur spurts,
Rock and stone, burn that hurts,
Treading lava, chains to yield,
Smoke in the air pollutes the blackened field,
Rock and ash, monsters fight,
Blood would boil, shadows of the night,
Horrors rising, eye would stare,
A foolish attempt to come and dare,
Legions mass, blacksmiths smack,
Fiendish pits, hellish black,
Spawning brood, born in the slime,
An unholy brood, a tainted crime,
Infestation all but clear,
Mindless ghouls unable to steer,
Such is the realm where darkness tread,
The foolish house of the restless dead.

Biting Sarcasm

Lori R. Lopez

It's raining teeth out there! Striking
a metal roof, colliding, bouncing, clattering
in a hail of stone throws, pebble blows,
a tinny resounding dash and ding of
hollow cascading staccato bites, as if
the heavens endeavor to munch through
the ceiling and rend me to bits—saw me to
a thousand halves—rip garish red ribbons
with fangs and incisors, nipping
and stripping to the bone!

I wasn't born here.

Frigid spasms quake me. The night
spills onto my abode its rampant assault,
a racketous bombarding fervor I have come
to dread in this stark brutal place where
no sense of order and calm may exist,
only fits and furies, violent psychedelic
breaks in the gray pall of a dismal atmosphere.
Flash-floods of misery open up in bursts
between days of maddening drought,
lightning strobes of intense disaster.

Into this hell I fell, out of a drowsy state.

Reason holds no sway, Reality force-fed
to dungeon beasts beneath a bristled demeanor
in this sordid space. Life a form of
stagnant death, withered and suffering aloud.
No explanation defines it, no purpose.
There is merely a chorus of noises like
shaking a glass jar of marbles and iron bolts,
while the how of a body's exile down the drain
of its domain whispers too quiet to interpret,
replaying over and over in one's head.

A bottomless storm of pellets.

Squeamish orbs screw tight against the gore
invoked by manic downpourings, bleak assails;
caustic raps, taps, claps and browbeats;
an echoing clamor in weather-drenched detail,
in nightmares carving me raw with fright
for the savageness of their appetite, their
ravenous riotous hurl. Strident, cacophonous,
drumming, pummeling like stones upon
steel, battering dreams of vessels
that cut waves through oily resonance.

From the din there is no rest, and no return.

Voyaging limits beyond measure, across
oceans of burgeoning billowing voids, currents
that crush the edges of coasts into eroded rubble
coating ivory beaches, glimmering reaches
of nethral shores on which the sands wandering
Infinity collect, heaped in cosmic corners.
Pulled like teeth out of mindless reveries, drawn
like grinning Helium-filled balloons on tethers
back to the underrealm, scattering the floor
of a subterrain that bates its ragged breath.

At dawn's break I sweep them up to save in jars.

If only rain could be soft, not hard as rock,
not peppering shacks and huts and keeping the
climate pulse, a tempest of sarcasm.
If only it could be candy-coated like gumballs,
sweet or sour to the taste, showering tooth
and gum. But wistful thoughts resemble
clouds, floating beyond touch—elusive wads
of smoke or lint that lack essential substance,
a silver-lining. Flimsier than Fool's Gold,
crumbling to worthless dust in your grasp.

Neath a pelting deluge, a perennial torrent . . .

Huddled with clenched knees, gritted molars;
at once cold and clammy to the depths of my gist,
the epitomes of saturated pits, I listen for
a Morse-Code meaning telegraphed from some
murky morbid trench at the base of the blackest sea:
a pearl of wisdom waiting to be discovered
in a Treasure Chest swallowed by mistral tides
of gloom as I hunker wide awake, aware of
the deafening percussive dance's descent
that my bludgeoned mind can never unhear.

The Universe has a strange sense of humor.

Lawrence Talbot

(with a nod, and, perhaps, an apology to E. A. Robinson)

Frank Coffman

Whenever Lawrence Talbot went to town,
The locals in the quaint shops looked at him.
He was a gentleman from sole to crown,
Well-favored (though sometimes his look was grim).
And he was always splendidly arrayed,
And he was always "human" when he spoke.
But Lawrence held a secret, was dismayed
Each monthnight when the frowning round moon broke
Through clouds or glared down from the clear, cold sky.
Those times, you see, Lawrence was "not quite right."
And someone in the drear of dark would die,
For, as a wolf-thing, Lawrence prowled the night.

Until, that day, a silver-handled cane—
Crushed down upon his skull—a werewolf's bane.

Twisted Grin

Ashley Dioses

Like coiling serpents in your chest,
Fear tightens as you claw and bleed.
Anxieties are at their best;
You pant as they begin to feed.

Your grinding bones are in your mind,
Yet still you make each socket pop
Your eyes right out from just behind
Those lids before they slip and drop.

Your fingernails still scratch the wall
As tears of blood trail down your face.
You stumble as you catch your fall;
The cooling crimson slows its race.

Your dreams will never see the light,
And every hope you have will fade.
As sun surrenders to the night,
Its freezing teeth sink sharp as blades.

Your deadened eyeballs stare in fear,
And yet you form a twisted grin.
From on the floor they each still peer,
And watch as you commit each sin.

The Vision

Ngo Binh Anh Khoa

The sky dims at the gathering of dark clouds,
Which swallows up the stars and slowly rends
The waxen moon; their festering presence shrouds
The slumberous world and all light apprehends.
All things are plunged unto a fathomless deep
Where not a sight the mortal eyes can see—
A realm submerged in shadows, where things creep
Unseen from nightmares to reality.
As my grim vision plays out, I could hear
The roaring waves there raging with the gale;
The cruise ship shakes, drowned in the screams of fear
That go unanswered midst this drifting cell.
Beneath the ship I gaze—into the black,
From which two massive orbs glare coldly back.

To Hypnos, Refuter of My Ego

Manuel Pérez-Campos

Thou relict of a pantheon extinct,
what sins have I incurred according to
thy ancient code that thou dost mercilessly
accost me through hazy nighted precinct
with shape not quite grasped of hooded fury,
till I envy those who lie not in their tomb
but walk in their shrouds, howling soullessly?
Why art thou intent on having me succumb
to the scars on thy leprous face and not
allow me to turn back just yet though pleading
for surcease? Mad thing immune to bartering:
what fulmination, now obscured from me
did I once invoke full against thee that
not even a thousand transmigrations
pursued against the dirge of ruined nations
hath served to keep each nightmare free of thee?

Mycophilia

DJ Tyrer

Her flesh yields spongily
Beneath my greedy fingers
As she lies unresisting
Upon a bed of mouldering leaves
Mouth open in a silent scream
An invitation for my questing tongue
Neither knowing nor caring
What cruel fate has placed her here
Passive and unresponsive
Plaything for my pleasure
Unseeing eyes blank and grey
With cataracts of a sort
And, as I enter her
She enters me
Carried upon moist breath
Spores drift languidly into my lungs
Eyes, stomach, loins
Infesting me, investing me
Until my frantic thrusting ceases
And, I grow still like her
Atop her, two bonded into a fungal one

Ave, Hell's Angel!

Carl E. Reed

To the Lord of Vice & Guarantor of Hell,
fierce fighting rebel-rouser of angelic hordes;
god of fire & frozen 9th-Circle realms,
beautiful Lucifer who dared to roar
e'en as truculence provoked a war
'gainst a tyrant of near-omniscient cosmic power
who counted eternal servitude just reward—
I pledge my wild soul at life's last hour.

I've bellowed, brawled, & howled in dim-lit bars,
made merry 'mongst cold-eyed killers, thieves, & whores;
driven thunder-mufflered trucks, & bikes, & cars,
ridden an armored chariot into war.
Vengeful fury upon the knock-kneed poured
when I challenged glib-tongued, craven-hearted cowards
who dared to proselytize, condemn, & bore—
I pledge my wild soul at life's last hour.

This world rewards the tiger, not the lamb;
it deals out death & horror as of old.
The meek: stampeded sheep; the kindly man
crushed under weight of violence, cant, & gold.
Therefore I shall not truckle: I shall be bold!—

winsome smile become a dark-browed glower.
O, I know this world is yours, Almighty Satan!

I pledge my wild soul at life's last hour.

& know that while I breathe I run amok—
to feast & drink, to laugh & fight & fuck!
O Noble, Bold Great Devil grant me power!
This wild soul is Yours at life's last hour.

The ballade is a French poetic form popular in the late 13th and 15th centuries, usually set to music. It comprises three eight-line verses and a four-line envoi typically addressed to a lord or master; the last line of each verse constituting a refrain.

A Means of Summoning

A Petrarchan Sonnet for M. R. James

Steven Withrow

Wry spirit, sessile as a pondweed, wake.
Sleep does not become you, nor the ebb
Of water through a water spider's web,
So large the diving bell could catch a snake
Where striders cross the wobble of the lake
To end life in a mallard's yellow nib,
The opposite of Eve from Adam's rib,
For any sense these correlations make.

In "A Warning to the Curious" you'll note
One squat martello tower on a bluff
(As troublous now as was it when you wrote)
Is, in its way, analogous enough
To how your soul has settled to rebuff
The notion that Old Scratch should hold your coat.

Mother of All Things

Christina Sng

One night, my eyeballs
Fell out of their sockets
And rolled under the bed,
Finding a litter of kittens
My shy cat had hidden.

I picked up my eyes,
Rinsed them gently
Through filtered water,
Popped them back in,
Adjusting them carefully.
Only then did I register
Those kittens weren't kittens
But mewling baby demons.
I carried them all out and
Popped them into the furnace.

In a month, they were fully grown,
Mottle-skinned and fire-charred.
I fed them with the nastiest folk
From all around town, and soon
They began to call me "Mom."

Igerna, Alone in Waning Moonlight

Geoffrey Reiter

"Tintagel is my last abode!"
    She sighed in darkness as the limpid moon
    Was robbed of all its glory far too soon,
And ravished by a rigid cloud.

And in that night, the surging waves
    Of spume and riptide battered hard the cliff
    And sieged the shoals like soldiers' spears, the stiff
Crest draining then into a cave.

A shiver wracked her body, and
    She bit her lip till bloody, stifling
    A cry. Such lonesome moaning rifling
About the walls, with near at hand

The mighty surge of Uther, king
    And tyrant, and his warriors, bronze and horn-
    Helmed, ill would aid her husband. Thus forlorn,
She gazed outside, still trembling

As those pure crystal eyes of hers,
    All bathed within their whites, fell on the tall
    And hungry turret, rising from the wall
As though it yearned for to immerse

Itself within the moon, which now
    Emerged, a mottled yellow in the sky.
    But wait! outside the door, a sound so nigh,
The sound of Cornwall's voice; but how

Could he have bested Uther's horde
    So soon? She pressed her ear against the hard,
    Unyielding wooden door, to catch each word
He spoke. Yet then, she thought, *My lord,*

Your voice is changed. It rages like
    The midday sun, like thunder that precedes
    A shaft of lightning; O, this new tone breeds
A fear in me. This voice could strike

A man to death, this sword could wreath
    A human heart in blood. So thought she, fear
    Then flooding her, till only could she hear
A drawn sword slide into its sheath.

Lord of Dreaming

Scott J. Couturier

He comes cloaked in many colors—
the Lord of Dreaming & Vision,
replete in vesture of celestial hoard.
Fair his guise, not of complexion but
countenance, face scoured by
astral ways of wayward reverie:
aspect worn to solemnity by Abyss's
chord—save, his garb adorned
with flecks of star-fire & æther,
arabesques of opal juxtaposed
to jaundiced amber of grotesque heft.
Moths of moonray feast on
his finery, pinions argent as they
wing him aloft: phosphor arrays his
vestment as he soars unbound by gravity's
bane, crowned by coronet of ulterior
suns, wily tenant of eternity's croft.
Dreams exude from his brow in
orbicular argosy, feet unfettered
as wind, mind unwound & bound
by no iron-shod archaic code:
all horizons his prefecture, odes
& oaths ardent on lips of flame,
majestic mastery of Beauty's cause,
every thew in vigorous accord

with Mystery's august auspice,
fantastic vistas unveiling to perennial
awe, each joint bejeweled with
Dreamer's desire, bijou of fairest
fane & blackest necromancer's
gold. The moon a suppliant of cold,
quiet light as he ascends into night,
tongue rampant with tales untold:
direst portent & Muse's ebullition,
whispers of ancestral decree &
quests of arcane quintessence,
coat fraught with coils of ethereal
aegis, bright coal from Promethean
forge out-cast, alight with augury,
free as dragon-kin in their eminent
element of forge-fire's helical flight.

Transubstantiator of the Finite

A Reflection on Virgil Finlay

Manuel Pérez-Campos

Through you I see the arch-deity quantum space,
progenitor of parallel worlds, erecting
with classical restraint of line, like a geometer
of Avernus, temples to itself. Bringer to
fantasque entelechy through phosphene pointillism
of the most ineffable moment of a pulp
tale: teach me to corrupt my cosmography by
imbruing a rogue cliff with a libido that
exudes colossal protofaces that can dream:
in your dharanas of lucid acherontic
monochrome rigor and subzero whim whirl
in equilibrium until a kamaloka
is sculpted in hierogamos with Eris. Nightmare
ayr entr'acte architect: exempt me from
ataraxia again: dissect with volte-face verve
the antique construct of solidity and scald
the ajna chakra with the kalpas' cataract.

Greetings from Krampus

Manuel Arenas

At this joyful time of year, full of festive reveling,
There is one whom you should fear if you're prone to deviling.
On the heels of blithe St. Nick, comes a fellow dark and wild,
Horned and beastly, like Old Nick, searching for a naughty child.
Cloven hoof and lolling tongue, with a basket on his back
Filled with wicked Alpine young, wailing at his switch's crack.
Lapping at their bleeding welts, their cries foment his dire thirst,
Heedless of their rueful guilt, doomed in demon's clasp they're curst.
After which they're borne to Hell, shackled in a clanking chain,
On a sled of ne'er-do-wells, never to be seen again!

In Central European folklore, Krampus represents the shadow side of the
Yule Time celebrations. An anthropomorphic goat/demon, he goes about
punishing naughty children with his switch, the worst of whom he binds in
chains, sticks in his basket, and drags to Hell. He is celebrated December 5-6,
and, in the Germanic countries, it has become customary to send
Krampuskarten (Krampus Cards) depicting lurid scenes of Krampus either
chastising children or frolicking with buxom Fräuleins. The common
salutation on these cards is *Gruß vom Krampus* (Greetings from Krampus).

Cetus

Wade German

Look there, out in the vast cerulean space surrounded only by itself: a
momentary island has emerged! It is Cetus, he of the finned ears,
webbed claws, and ship-devouring jaws! His enormous scales of dazzling
aquamarine glitter like a thousand shields in the afternoon sunlight! But
as we see his titanic tail-fin re-enter the blue element, let us consider an
amazing truth: while rising through unfathomed leagues to eventually
swallow a cold tonnage of krill near the surface, he has suffered the
harpoon-like stroke of an intellectual pang: Why does existence
perpetuate itself in this manner? The thought is like a barnacle that
stubbornly roots itself to his brain; he is unable to scrape it off against
the submarine mountains. But he is soon comforted by the soothing
songs of the parasites that infest his quintupled sets of gills. It is they
who lift him from the beetling, coral-encrusted shelfs that are his morbid
fits; the impenetrably black abyssals of his pendulous moods. Sometimes,
he also finds solace in the tender, empathic telepathies of the
bioluminescent jellyfishes, or in the benevolent communications so
sagely offered by the giant clams. But when his gigantic hearts (there are
many beating in his body), momentarily inundated with extreme
palpitations of joy, begin to shudder and sink once again into the
lugubrious slime of melancholy, we wonder with him: will he forever
roam the seas without purpose? Do not suffer such cogitations, O Cetus!
Those incorrigible perturbations will soon cease! For at this very
moment, the oceanic voice of the Great Progenitor of the sharks, the
whales, and the squids has summoned you to service—and at last, you
will find meaning in his call!

Shadowlands

Leigh Blackmore

My head is filled with skeleton trees;
My thoughts are full of skeleton keys;
Trees nod their skulls like skeleton men;
The road is rough and stardark again.

Lovesick, I see you stand still and fair,
Mired deep in mud. With black branches bare,
Tall trees glow bright and unearthly-hued;
Dim peaks rise far, with shadows imbued.

Your hair is twined with skeleton bones;
You dream of kings on skeleton thrones;
Your dress of shadows conceals your form;
Your face, anguish-lit, is split by storm.

I feel the beat of skeleton heart;
I drag my feet. There is some black art
At work; I feel its skeleton bane
Pour forth to waste my pitiful brain.

My ears are filled with skeleton cries;
Your lips, they part; 'neath menacing skies
I see my fate; you raise your clawed hands—
"Beware, beware, the dread Shadowlands!"

A Ghostly Shade of Oil

Oliver Smith

Into the world the painter danced them.
She formed, with fingertips and flat knife,
a second Giaconda in the sunrise;
her twilight iris glazed in the dark honey
of velvet brushwork. The artist's alchemy
ignited reflections in her hair and eyes;
thought conjured her from the dimmed light
of lost hallways, out of un-empty rooms.

Reborn: a picture before the easel;
from out of haunted attics, spirits drawn,
sketched, and painted: her mirror-twin,
Spartan Helen, beneath the crimson moon;
Lilith: new-made; made flesh over bone,
worked with rag and brush: fat over thin.
Her scaled skin glimmered as in Earth's dawn
haunted by the future ghost of feral Eve.

She waltzed, down to the timeless sea;
and weakened under the connoisseurs gaze:
Astarte returned to red crumbling rust;
to the pale chalk hills, returned Salome;
to air-rotted lead, returned Persephone.
Now the wolf hunts in the turpentine pines;
in linseed like asphodel reaps a painter's shade;
fugitive in the light of faded centuries.

His Dark Light Shines

Allan Rozinski

Flanked by the remains
of sere wheat and rye shorn short,
a long field of desiccated corn husks
that dance to and fro to the lowing wind's gusts,
dry stalks rustling and rattling a warning,
an ancient, funereal song.

The rite inspired by the harvester of life,
reaping produce from all, budding to ripe,
where the god of sterility then lays claim to the earth
and smothers the heat and warmth that gives birth,
to drain what life remains from the veins of the soil,
now turned cold and hard and unforgiving.

In the midst of the field stands a makeshift cross,
a corpse lies prostrate at the foot of its base,
on the rood itself hangs a sinister sentinel
seeming to peer skyward, waiting for a sign
from somewhere beyond the descending dusk,
out of the dreaded, unfathomable design.

The alien darkness suffuses the form
and works its effect amidst the gathering storm,
animating the puppet as if raised from the dead,
the stuffed surrogate of a man lifts its head,
its purpose no longer to haunt beast and bird,
but instead to spread its blight outward unto the world.

The Empty House

Josh Maybrook

It sits upon a lonely plot of ground,
A dwelling once inhabited until
Its owners passed from sight; now all around,
A sense of quiet strangeness lingers still.
Its attic dormers rise, bizarrely angled,
To meet the hazy autumn's falling leaves,
As tentacles of ivy climb entangled
Upon its cornices and slanted eaves.
At night, the townsfolk daren't venture near,
For then a ghostly aura subtly falls;
And in an upper window lights appear
Exposing spiderwebs on peeling walls;
And weird dæmonic shadows seem to loom
Inside that solitary attic room.

Bridal Bower

David Barker

The one he loved was laid within the vault,
Her white-gloved hands across her breast were placed.
Draped in a gown beguiling but yet chaste:
In form and deed, a maiden without fault.
And then the tomb door shut, and darkness ruled.
The unclean horde assembled in her crypt.
In mockery of Love, the bride was stripped,
And all her ghoulish grooms leered long and drooled.

Well fed and sated of their lusts, they fled.
Behind they left bare bones and shredded silk,
Reminders of the maid he once adored.
When told she'd perished and would never wed,
He yearned to touch once more her skin like milk.
Within her tomb, they found his body, gored.

Arch Wizardry, the Glorious Opulence of St. Toad

(by a Disciple of St. Toad, writ in the year c. 1302 or 1320 C.E.)

Charles Lovecraft

"Beware St. Toad's cracked chimes!" I heard him scream . . .

Take note, young wight,
    Fine-feathered twit,
Such morbid sense
    As I have writ.

I passed a law
    That any man
Which looked a toad
    Would find a ban;

For none there should
    Look like St. Toad;
An' if they did
    I wrote an ode,

And called *Them* up,
    From realms below
And all around,
    To eat and grow.

I've crucified
        Such toads of men;
Such loads of them
        Pushed in a pen,

And seen their heads
        Removed as quick,
By nighted things
        As with a flick,

As if the swipe
        Of some vast tongue,
Had loathsome borne
        From all the dung,

And *multiplied*
        From holy ground,
The wormy pores,
        Misshapen round,

And whisked their lives
        Away in time.
The tongues returned
        To their black slime.

And now the earth,
    That wormy *dirt*
Which wriggles here,
    Knows our weak hurt.

While somewhere tossed
    In radiance,
Black opulence,
    St. Toad shall prance,

And whinny close,
    With claws curled vast
Upon his chest,
    Blow the long blast,

The summoning blast,
    Keen as the wind
Of cosmic space,
    To kill all kind.

The Burning Man

Steven Withrow

The burning man is after me;
He ate the forest, tree by tree.
He's slim of limb and thin of skin.
He rings the flaming orchard in
His arms of Agent Orange, and
A swarm of aphids in his hand.

The burning man has eaten well,
And by his leavings I can tell
He favors cherry over pear;
He flings the pits, a browsing bear;
But even though he's sated, he
Will clear another plate for me.

The burning man is instant blight:
An ash-black thumb, a torch to light
The stubble fields in Stygian mist
Like kindling for an arsonist.
I can't deter him, nor assuage;
He hunts for pleasure, not for rage.

The burning man is growing wise
To where I run. His mantis eyes
Are now protruding to the sea—
Too soon he will be done with me—
Up the headland, down the pier:
His wicker crown is here, is here!

Dancing Before Azathoth

Darrell Schweitzer

Came the demon
into the darkness of my dream.
Spake the demon,
"Rise up, take my hand,
and I will show thee
terrors never before imagined,
wonders never described,
secrets never written,
even in the blasphemous tomes of the mad."
So we plunged together into that place
beyond the confines of the grave,
where flesh and bones are sloughed off
and the spirit breaks free to soar.
We waded, stars splashing
about our ankles like foam,
and we dove down to where stone-faced gods
slept and dreamed and waited.
How we fled in terror
from the opening of their eyes!
All stars, all worlds, all dust of creation,
the very tombs of the gods
seemed no more than scum
on the surface of a greater sea,
through which we plummeted now,
in helpless fascination and despair,

until we circled and danced before
the black throne of Azathoth.
From this dream,
neither my prideful, foolish demon,
nor my likewise foolish self,
can ever dare awaken,
lest the lord of that black throne should rise up
and follow us back into the waking world,
and devour it all.

The Unknown

Lori R. Lopez

That scuttle and clicking of
                    claws in the night
How creepy and dramatic
                is such a fright

Peering into darkness quite poorly equipped
To explain the reason I stumbled and tripped

Or whose breath I discern on
                    the nape of my neck
Why emotions and nerves
                are a twisted wreck

Do you think you can imagine the unfathomable fear
When something uncertain scrambles near

A legion of talons,
               a myriad of limbs
Scraping while thrashing
                  like an army of grims

And you're faced with confronting the unforeseen
In nary a glimmer, not the slightest sheen

Of a candle's light—
              a warm lantern's glow?

How terrible it is
                    to quake and not know

What slithers beyond our Comfort Zone
The space where we feel less or most alone

Confined by the Dark like
                            a pantomime box
Yet how we now crave
                        a safe place with locks!

I can tell you firsthand I should not be here
To risk losing parts that are held quite dear

The Unknown is always
                        not far behind
You can hear it, sense it,
                            turn around and find . . .

What you least expected, you hadn't suspected
A dreadful surprise, and you're so unprotected!

I will never forget
                    what I refused to see—
The something or nothing
                        that won't get me!

Runestone

Ann K. Schwader

Beyond the uttermost of Thule's wastes,
a many-angled mystery arose
before the light of history. Encased
in primal mist, its mass awaited those
who worshipped nameless chaos-spawn—& bore
their random shapings. Night by moonless night,
they scribed each surface thick with runes, adored
their gods with bloodied claws until the blight
of them receded from our world. Now few
but madmen & epigraphers still dare
this desolation. Straining to undo
each knotwork of lost prophecies, they stare
uncomprehending, fated not to learn
these secrets left for Those who shall return.

Galactic Cellars, Unhinged

Maxwell I. Gold

Where nebulous horizons curled underneath arms of breathing starlight, there laid a menagerie of stars. In the fading blackness of an ancient dark I saw the vacuous night, bleeding with murky wonders unlike anything ever imagined or conceived by the most lucid of men. Caught in webs of dust and shadow, yellow stars cried oceans of liquid dreams, soaking the purple firmaments under their quantum tears. I felt each drop one after another like starquakes, dripping from the rusty gates of a broken place long since dead. Manic fantasies and pyroclastic nightmares soon took flight on the backs of giant winged Naigoths, shattering the last pitiful remnants of those galactic cellars, coated with a sinister mirth, floating in my thoughts.

I found myself traveling along a broken road, lost, where skies cracked under the heavy weight of a thousand planets as that nebulous horizon waned. My fingers dragged over a piece of parchment attempting to capture the reactionary consequences of a dying race, blasting forth from the molten skies. Shaky, unnerved, and broken, I penned the last words of an age, the final page in an era of post-truth and rampant sycophantism as the last drops of sea water boiled from the earth, sucked into a dry atmosphere; the clouds settling, spilling onto the glassy planetoid and liquid dreams cooling my consciousness. Ice and rock preserving the last precious atoms of terror, where nebulous horizons curled underneath arms of breathing starlight.

Amongst the Flowers

(For Clark Ashton Smith in Pacific Grove)

Scott J. Couturier

Bending low over
calla lily, waxleaf, azalea, anemone:
a weather-stained beret
& the wind-chime jangle of keys.

Human, he tills
in the rich, black, loaming earth:
fey eyes dart up,
furtive & fiery with intracosmic birth.

He gets a small fee
for his work amongst the inflorescence:
Adompha's servant,
life-blood blued with bardic essence.

True Poet, he digs
& clips, plants & uproots & dead-heads:
a Promethean titan
tenderly tending to mundane flower-beds.

His name is unknown
to most: "That odd, queer, fire-eyed man."
His spade is blooded:
allegiance owed to no terrestrial clan.

Human shit-ilization
roils & toils as he tends to the blooms.
No neon haunts his mind,
but incandescent vapors, arch-opiate fumes—

Bright golden
light of wonder & terror his marrows suffuse.
Gently, he pots
rosemary for winter: long-quiescent his Muse.

Yet, the Emperor dreams
such beauty as to blind the novitiate's eye.
Old man dirt-grubbing:
Seer of sphereless marvels & sidereal sky.

The Dearg-Due[*]
An Irish Legend of Horror

(a long-line ballad)

Frank Coffman

After a thousand years have swept the Earth,
Her given name is lost to history.
Her surname, her evil husband's, and her peasant love's—
All, all are gone in mists of mystery.

But the tale tells she was most beautiful
Of all the maids 'round County Waterford.
What's more, the most gracious, pious, kind
Of all fair maidens who lived life by The Word.

She was of noble class, but Fate befell
That she a handsome peasant lad should love.
True partner to her soul: kind, loving, pure.
But her Father would not their blessèd match approve.

Through greed, he gave his daughter's gentle hand
To an evil, cruel, much older wealthy lord.
And, while the Father reveled in the bride price,
Her wicked husband all pious vows ignored.

---

[*] (pronounced DAH-ruhg DU-ah). It means "red-blood sucker"

He tortured her in body and in mind,
He kept her captive in his castle tower.
She would be his alone to touch, defile,
And bear the brunt of his most evil power.

His twisted mind brought forth a horrid plan.
He lusted to see her fair skin cut and bleed!
And from this torture and this bondage foul
She prayed each night that she be somehow freed.

She prayed her peasant love might learn some way
To find and rescue her and take her hence
From this foul fiend, this tower of torture vile—
But prayed in vain. There was no recompense.

She did not know that help would never come;
She did not know her true love lay long dead.
The ungodly lord of her misery had made sure
The peasant lad was slain the day they wed.

Slowly her heart's Hope dwindled to Despair.
She took the only means left for release.
Through agonizing steps she starved herself,
But, with her death, her spirit found no peace.

That spirit had been twisted by her pains,
Her mind in torment lost her pious Faith.
Her last vow was a vengeance terrible,
She too would seek blood as a vampire wraith!

Remembering the pious maid she'd been
The villagers that first night piled no stones—
As custom had it—on the poor girl's grave,
To ward off rising of the new-dead bones.

And so, she rose, the dreaded *Dearg-Due,*
Not only spirit, but the wasted body whole,
Ghastly and gaunt, but able to still disguise
With tempting beauty to enthrall the soul.

Transformed to a thief of blood, a threat to life,
She favors youthful prey, especially young men.
They are lured by her siren song in sleepless night
To her gravesite—not seen alive again.

She keeps them with her as she once was kept.
The lucky ones are soon bled dead and dry;
Those whom she "favors" have a more horrid fate:
She savers slow—in agony they die!

Those who go missing all that region round,
Those who become mysteriously ill,
Those children who die most inexplicably,
'Tis thought *"the insatiate one"* will have her fill.

And so a vampire thing plagues Ireland's land.
The Dearg-Due's call still echoes through the night.
Beneath the cold moon's light, o'er wood and wold,
Still sounds the keening of this wretched wight.

Fairies from the Twilight Forest

Christina Sng

In the twilight forest
Fairies gather once a year
To celebrate midsummer
With the sacrifice of monsters.

At dusk, their conjurers open
A shimmering blue portal
To the world of humans and
Take the worst of their kind:

The ones who terrorize
Their children with knives,
Slaughtering these monsters
Beneath the starry moonlight,

Letting their languid blood
Seep deep into the soil
To stir the saplings alive,
The desiccated bodies left

For wild animals to devour
So they know the taste of evil
When the day comes
And the time arrives

For all forest folk
To gather and fight,
And take back the world
From the monsters outside.

Lycanthropic Howl

Carl E. Reed

Is the eternal truth man's fighting soul
Wherein the beast ravens in his own avidity?
                    —Richard Eberhart

'Twas blinding rage & fury stoked white-hot
that gnashed my teeth, balled fingers into fists
long ere the upright wolf, werewolf begot—
it seemed I saw but dimly through black mists
of seething hate & killing woe: this Earth
marked & mauled the beast with rending claws;
bald babe become a child of cruel mirth
& fierce upholder of amoral law:
All is permitted if one have but strength!
I roam dark woodlands now by glowing moon
whose wintry silvered spears illume dense lengths
of fragrant pine & black loam; I typhoon
with hell-froth spatter foam & revel howls
red thrashing meat 'neath cold-eyed, circling owls.

Eternal Night

Geoffrey Reiter

If in the smear of stars across the nights
We see the salt-sea, gutted corpse stretched out
Of Tiamat, dead dragon, and the lights
That twinkle are her glinting scales that spout
Their beastly blood on that horizon, where,
Past gloam, the maw of Apep yawns, his fangs
Agape at Re and Set, prepared to tear
Into the dream of dawns; if chaos hangs
Beyond the Gorgon-guarded ford and all
The cosmos bear its ghastly stench, as though
Leviathan had belched with acrid gall
And proud disgust the galaxies, and no
Sweet-scented breath brood o'er the sea,
How shall we live amid the damned debris?

Spleen (III)

(after Baudelaire)

DJ Tyrer

If I were king of the city beyond the lake
I wonder what course my life would take?
Young and feminine, yet old and masculine
Willing to indulge in every conceivable sin
Yet uncheered by any such debauchery
Nor even distracted by insanity
Nor the peculiar antics of my jester
And, entertainments of the Falconer, Hastur
And, when with courtesans, I would wince
Their attentions undesired by this prince
No matter how sweet and delicate their bloom
Their embrace is chill just like a tomb
Not even when the ball with all my friends
The pale-masked Stranger attends
Nothing can stir me from my apathy
My soul-deep, mind-dulling lethargy
No, if I were king of the city beside the lake
Ere long, my own life I should take.

The Dark Descent

Ngo Binh Anh Khoa

My skin's whipped numb by harsh winds in the night
As I race through strange streets in darkness drowned,
Draped thinly in the full moon's withering light,
Which quietly fades when black clouds gather round.
The rending air tears through frail quivering leaves
That flail and wail around my buzzing ears;
My chest, throughout my frenzied running, heaves
As I strive to outpace my festering fears.
In vain I try, for never far behind,
I hear the growls that ride the roaring gales
From things that I, by vengeance rendered blind,
Have summoned from the foul depths of nine Hells.
My shadow, yawning, stretching, suddenly shrieks,
And midst that formed abyss, my horror peaks.

Memories of Another Country

Manuel Pérez-Campos

"An entire class of susceptibilities, and a gift connected with them,—of
no great richness or value, but the best I had,—was gone from me."
                    —Nathaniel Hawthorne, "The Custom-House"

Whether in Boone's canoe Kentuck, the dizzies
of the Mississip, or the hollyhocks of the great
purchase, a piece of America is still Arcady,
and in dialogue with that part of the submind
that manufactures nightly, like a banshee,
the terror of a spirit truth: Here no locomotive
that puts the shortgrass prairie into stoked smoke
linear gear: Here no faultline bison slain for
slaying's sake: Here only a linking of your will
to fireflies and to a setting out with johnnycake
and sack of apple seeds to become a servitor
of boundlessness: Here your doppelgänger,
wiser than you, being tamed by the promissory
of thunderhead-primed stretches and sundered
chrysalis: These are the mysteries I grew up with.

Classic Reprints

The Fairy Rings

John Clare

I

Here on the greensward, 'mid the old mole-hills,
  Where ploughshares never come to hurt the things
Antiquity hath charge of,—Fear instils
  Her footsteps, and the ancient fairy rings
Shine black, and fresh, and round—the gipsy's fire,
  Left yesternight, scarce leaves more proof behind
Of midnight sports, when they from day retire,
  Than in these rings my fancy seems to find
Of fairy revels; and I stoop to see
  Their little footmarks in each circling stain,
And think I hear them, in their summer glee,
  Wishing for night, that they may dance again;
Till shepherds' tales, told 'neath the leaning tree
While shunning showers, seem Bible-truths to me—

II

Aye, almost Scripture-truths!—My poorer mind
Grows into worship of these mysteries,
While Fancy doth her ancient scrolls unbind
That Time hath hid in countless centuries;
And when the morning's mist doth leave behind
The fungus round, and mushroom white as snow,
They strike me, to romantic moods inclined,
As shadows of things modelled long ago:
Halls, palaces, and marble columned domes,
And modern shades of fairies' ancient homes,
Erected in these rings and pastures still,
For midnight balls and revelry; and then
Left like the ruins of all ancient skill,
To wake the wonder of mere common men.

[From John Clare's *The Rural Muse* (London: Whittaker & Co., 1835), 164–65.]

The Dark Château

Walter de la Mare

In dreams a dark château
    Stands ever open to me,
In far ravines dream-waters flow,
    Descending soundlessly;
Above its peaks the eagle floats,
Lone in a sunless sky;
Mute are the golden woodland throats
    Of the birds flitting by.

No voice is audible. The wind
    Sleeps in its peace.
No flower of the light can find
    Refuge 'neath its trees;
Only the darkening ivy climbs
    Mingled with wilding rose,
And cypress, morn and evening, time's
    Black shadow throws.

All vacant, and unknown;
    Only the dreamer steps
From stone to hollow stone,
    Where the green moss sleeps,
Peers at the river in its deeps,
    The eagle lone in the sky,
While the dew of evening drips,
    Coldly and silently.

Would that I could press in!
    Into each secret room;
Would that my sleep bright eyes could win
    To the inner gloom;
Gaze from its high windows,
    Far down its mouldering walls,
Where amber-clear still Lethe flows,
    And foaming falls.

But ever as I gaze,
    From slumber soft doth come
Some touch my stagnant sense to raise
    To its old earthly home;
Fades then that sky serene;
    And peak of ageless snow;
Fades to a paling dawn-lit green,
    My dark château.

[From Walter de la Mare's *The Listeners and Other Poems* (New York: Henry Holt & Co., 1916), 59–60.]

Reviews

Three Poets, Three Visions

S. T. Joshi

K. A. OPPERMAN. *Past the Glad and Sunlit Season: Poems for Halloween.* Preface by Lisa Morton. Salem, OR: Jackanapes Press, 2020. 123 pp. $15.99 tpb.

THOMAS TYRRELL. *The Poor Rogues Hang.* Kenilworth, UK: Mosaïque Press, 2020. 53 pp. £4.99/$6.49 pb.

FARAH ROSE SMITH. *Oblivion Dances.* New York: Wraith Press, 2020. $6.78 pb.

Three poets who have appeared in *Spectral Realms* have issued new books of poetry, and each of the books contains matter of interest. At a minimum, they reveal the manner in which each poet's unique vision dictates the subject-matter and even the verse-forms they have chosen. Poetry, perhaps the most intense mode of expression in all the arts, may also engender the most distinctive *manner* of expression, intimately connected as it is to the poet's sensibility and outlook.

K. A. Opperman burst onto the weird poetry scene with the scintillating volume *The Crimson Tome* (Hippocampus Press, 2015), and since then he has been a dominant figure in the field—a key member of the Crimson Circle, made up of his fellow poets Ashley Dioses, Adam Bolivar, and D. L. Myers. In *Past the Glad and Sunlit Season* he has written a thematically unified volume that, on the surface, may hint at monotony: after all, how much can one say about Halloween without treading the same ground over and over again? But Opperman's book is refreshingly variegated in both subject and meter—it is a compelling volume from beginning to end.

In a surprisingly long and fascinating introduction, Opperman spells out his own lifelong obsession with Halloween. As children, of course, we all like the holiday for the abundance of candy we are given; but even as a youth Opperman began sensing the deeper and more sinister aspects of the season. This realization was augmented when he began growing pumpkins himself, as an outgrowth of his membership in an informal group, the Order of the Thinned Veil. The care and attention needed to grow pumpkins from seed to fruition was a profound experience: "I found myself becoming ever more in tune with the cycle of the seasons, the Wheel of the Year, that primal, pastoral foundation on which all of our seasonal celebrations are but haunted way-posts." He was so bold as to begin celebrating "The Religion of Halloween," writing one or more poems each year to commemorate the season. This book is the welcome result.

What first strikes us in *Past the Glad and Sunlit Season* is, indeed, the emphasis on the season itself—the melancholy time of falling leaves, which point to the onset of winter. "Waiting for October" is a poignant evocation of autumn ("I'm waiting for the gloaming / When gourds and candles glow / To guide the spirits roaming / From lands we cannot know"). "The Jack-o'-Lantern Trail" has a similar burden ("Grim Jack-o'-lanterns light the shadowed way, / Each carven visage different from the last; / They flicker over carpets of decay / Where walk the restless spirits of the past"). And there is acute terror in the season, too as "Path of the Will-o'-th'-Wisp" attests:

> Mine is the way that no other has gone,
> Pathless my footstep, but pointed my tread;
> Mine is the way between twilight and the dawn,
> Where wander the lost and the dead.

One of the most effective poems in the book—although only one of many—is "The Wraith," singled out by Lisa Morton in her preface. What is the wraith that the protagonist senses "as haunted winds told tales of yesterday"?

> Its woeful features crumbled from its face,
> Leaving a screaming skull to take their place.

And of that wraith of eld soon not a trace
Was left on misty air.

"The Ballad of Lantern Jack" would appear to bear the influence of
Adam Bolivar, who has made the weird ballad his chosen specialty.
Opperman acknowledges that the poem was written "After Jason
McKittrick's account of a New Jersey legend," but the ballad form of the
poem seems to be a tip of the hat to Bolivar (who is the co-dedicatee of
the book, along with Derrick Hussey).

Past the Glad and Sunlit Season is also deft in fusing romance, even
eroticism, with the weird, as "Masque Macabre" and "Love Beyond the
Grave" are sufficient to prove. "The Clown Witch" finds terror in a
carnival, while "Hymn to the Great Pumpkin" exhibits the strangeness of
that seemingly harmless gourd:

We've chosen you to hold the Samhain Flame,
And guard against the ghosts that haunt this night.
Yours is the weirdly dancing, eldritch light
Wherein is mystery without a name.

In assessing this book, it is impossible to ignore the superb book
design of its publisher, Daniel V. Sauer, who has provided a bountiful
supply of his own illustrations all throughout the volume. Jackanapes
Press deserves the support of all lovers of weird poetry: the
advertisements for forthcoming titles found at the back of this book
suggest a keen editorial eye and a devotion to the genre that are more
than admirable in these challenging times.

Thomas Tyrrell's *The Poor Rogues Hang* is a book of a very
different order. Focusing on pirate lore and legendry (the author, in a
brief "historical note," indicates that many of the poems found their
subject-matter in the 1724 volume *The General History of the Robberies and
Murders of the Most Notorious Pirates*, attributed to a Captain Charles
Johnson), Tyrrell has written a succession of ballads, lyrics, and even a
play that all explore the problematical status of the pirate in history and
society. Many of the poems are, perhaps, not quintessentially weird or
supernatural, but they are all engaging and compelling. Here we find
poems about female pirates ("Anne Bonny to Captain Johnson," "Of
Mary Read"). In the latter, Mary appears to be addressing the Anne of

the former poem: "I would still be fighting / for King George in Flanders, my sex unthought of, / you in marriage chained to a sailor-husband, / oceans between us").

"Of Captain Vane" is a lengthy poem about a captain shipwrecked on a deserted island. He is on the point of being rescued by his former colleagues—but they are now "licensed privateer[s]" (i.e., pirates who have been officially commissioned by a government to sail the seas and capture or destroy enemy vessels), and his former first mate, Holford, doesn't trust him; so he leaves Vane ashore, where he will be hanged:

> So Vane is left, alone in night,
> to make whatever peace he might.
> and all that night, in fevered dreams,
> he writes and spasms, swears, blasphemes,
> curses his fate but nothing seems
> to be of any use.

"A Cilician Pirate, 57 BC" reminds us that piracy is a profession that extends back centuries: the Romans were brutally efficient in eliminating pirates from the Mediterranean. "A Frightful Ballad of the Third Lord Boyce" does venture into the supernatural, telling of how that nobleman met a ship bearing his dead father and his crew. "Of Captain Davies" is a rousing ballad, but one that also emphasizes how pirates (and the authorities opposed to them) were both deeply involved in the slave trade.

Of Captain Teach is a short play in flawless iambic pentameter blank verse. Teach is "the terror of the Outer Banks" (i.e., of North Carolina), and two sailors discuss his ambiguous status in a tavern:

> Why, when my knee is paining me of nights
> I wish him truly damned as man can be.
> Yet other times I fancy he escaped
> The devil's clutches by some scurvy trick,
> Clawed off a lee shore by the Cape of Hell
> To sail with Avery and Henry Morgan
> Into the sea of legends—damn his eyes!

The most famous pirate of them all, Captain Kidd, is the subject of one of the final poems in the book, "Of Captain Kidd." Here the ghost of that baleful figure protests that he has been unjustly treated by history and legend, as he started out as a "pirate hunter" who was unfairly hanged for piracy.

The Poor Rogues Hang is a slim volume, but one that displays admirable richness and variety while maintaining a unity of theme and subject. The poet has, in other work, already demonstrated that his poetic range is far broader than what this booklet indicates, and we hope that more of his work can find its way between the covers of a book.

As for *Oblivion Dances* by Farah Rose Smith (whose "The Germ of the Earth" appeared in *Spectral Realms* for Winter 2017), I imagine I am a bit too conventional and rational to appreciate it. This slim volume of untitled quasi-haiku or imagist fragments (it is unclear how many there are, since the book is not paginated), ranging from a single line to eight or nine, evidently relies on creating in the reader a sense of the power of individual words or phrases to generate fleeting impressions of various sorts; but to my mind they are a bit too ephemeral to be effective. Some of them verge on weirdness. Here, for example, is an entire poem:

> A sweet gaze
> Sadness and pain
> A ghoul in my head
> Drunken broken

Here is another:

> Graveyards
> Somewhere in the depths
> Her lips
> Sweet
> The woods
> Secret
> This hour
> Horror

To be sure, these are all interesting experiments in form, but one would like to see Smith write (as indeed she has done elsewhere) more substantial and coherent work that might create a more lasting impression.

Bring Out Your Dead and Other Speculations

Donald Sidney-Fryer

STEVEN WITHROW. *The Bedlam Philharmonic and Other Poems.* Falmouth, MA: Steven Withrow, 2020. 49 pp. $6.99 tpb.
FRANK COFFMAN. *Black Flames and Gleaming Shadows: A New Collection of Speculative Poetry.* Elgin, IL: Mind's Eye Publications, 2020. 210 pp. $14.95 tpb.
OLIVER SHEPPARD. *Thirteen Nocturnes.* Dallas, TX: Ikonograph Press, 2018. 258 pp. $13.00 tpb.

Three volumes of exceptional weird poetry have come to hand this winter and early spring, two but recently published, the third in 2018.

For those readers not overwhelmed by the current worldwide pandemic, these three exceptional books may provide a further frisson, that is, since late 2019 and early 2020, more or less coincident with the epidemic. In April 2020 we spoke with a close friend in New York City, then the U.S. epicenter of the novel coronavirus, COVID-19, where 10,000 persons or more died from the disease. The special friend reassured us that people in public places, indoors or out, are wearing masks as advised, and keeping six feet or more away from one another, as most intelligent people appear to be doing. The same friend also reassured us that corpses had not piled up at street corners or along the sidewalks. Horse-drawn wagons were not circulating along the boulevards and avenues with the funereal drivers calling in stentorian terms, "Bring out your dead" for collection as in times not so long past.

About a year ago, we received here at our new home on Cape Cod a package of poems from Steven Withrow residing in Falmouth, then a stranger but now known to us as poet, writer, and teacher. The poems mostly concerned dark fantasy, horror, the supernatural. We read and acknowledged them, and we had hoped that we would meet him at the NecronomiCon of August 2019 in Providence, Rhode Island, but that meeting did not happen. Then, in March of 2020, Steven mailed us a copy of his first collection. His poetry seems to us original and very well crafted, and using a variety of forms with skill and finesse. They also demonstrate a nice sense of irony, humor, and wit. This volume marks an auspicious debut, and we hasten to felicitate Steven on his achievement. Bravo! Albeit slender, it packs a lot into it, as well as a real punch.

We can only note what S. T. Joshi states on the back cover. "This is a strikingly impressive book. the poems are by turns haunting, grim, poignant, and thought-provoking; but they also display Steven Withrow's effortless mastery of verse forms and of that telling word or phrase." From page 41 we cite the following poem as a typical example from Steven's pen.

Meerwich Library

Meerwich Library has a lowest level
Where stairs and elevators do not go.
The superstitions might suppose a devil
Had dug its lair there, but the keepers know
No purpose for that story. The architects,
Dross, Mountebank & Mori, had fixed a trap
In the upper floor that, edgewise, intersects,
When opened with the buildings deepest gap
Accessible by rope or by a lunge
Into a black that lamplight can't expunge.

For ninety years, the sharpest intellects
From Angstrom University have tried to map
Wellsprings of tht space, and their work rejects

The "wormhole postulation" held by Rapp
And Thorton. Here's a counterquote from Neville:
"Our instruments and observations show
The Meerwich Athenaeum's lowest level—
Impervious to any shine or glow,
Repellent as any kleptolucent sponge—
Is bottomless, and nowhere we should plunge."

And we can't resist quoting the last paragraph of "The Beaching" of some strange sea-creature, a "fine miraculous" entity. This piece is the last in the selection in the book before the "Notes on Forms."

Our eyes traced down the delicate line of her body, now reclining on her side, to her physical completion, her once-powerful tail, as fine and natural as the broad caudal appendage of a bottlenose dolphin, or a lady toothed whale.

That last represents a neat, fastidious bit of natural history, another indication of Steven's linguistic and rhythmic adroitness.

Unlike so many poets, if not most, restricted to the one string on their lyre of horror or the supernatural, Frank Coffman—otherwise Franklin Coffman II—has many strings to his lyre, as indicated on the title page of his latest collection: "Poems of the Weird, Horrific, Supernatural, Fantastic, Science Fictional, Metapoetical and Traditional." His major collection, *The Coven's Hornbook,* alerted us to a major new voice in imaginative poetry, a collection even larger than this, and no less diversified. And that says a great deal right there. he already has more than several books of poetry (authored or edited) to his name, and has already more than several books in progress. As anyone who has experienced his work knows for a fact, Frank is a master poet, a wizard of rime, meter, and form. Truly a grand and glorious traditionalist! Appropriately he ends this latest collection with a "glossary of forms" that runs to twenty well-packed pages. Clearly he is no cheapskate!

Anyone who knows Frank's work in depth knows how near impossible it is to cite a typical poem of his facture. All that we can do is to cite almost at random this sci-fi specimen as follows:

The Cyborg Dilemma

(an irregular sonnet)

Beyond that world that's new—not brave—
When there are countless clones of you;
After when folks wondered what might come to view,
And that age-old world of mating we did not save—
Might it not be that the cradle *is* the grave,
When brain and body meld in biomechanics,
After the suppression of initial panics,
When we finally decide to leave old Plato's cave?
Won't that sun be too bright for our "infirm delight?"
Those eyes won't see the same sky's blue,
But other spectra, strange—though true.
Will they put star-scan grids upon the NIGHT?
Mind's output to cold device won't be the toll,
But the machine's input to the human soul.

As a special bonus Frank has a lovely, often subtle sense of humor deployed throughout many of the poems, so lovingly crafted and presented. We are constantly finding in these almost 200 pages, including the erudite and instructive "glossary of forms," much to engage us and give us pause. We surely recommend this collection to the adventurous reader, who shall find much here as cause for discovery and exploration, and not less for cerebration as well as an unique sense of liberty or liberation.

The last book under perusal and review comes to us courtesy of a great and good friend in Manhattan. Otherwise we would have remained ignorant of it and the author-poet. And Oliver Sheppard and his finely calibrated collection *Thirteen Nocturnes* cause us the same problem as Frank Coffman's collection: a large collection and many poems of uniformly high craftsmanship, not to mention creativity. It is hard to know, to identify, that which seems most apt or typical to quote in full.

But this full and generous collection contains more than the "Thirteen Nocturnes." The other three sections that follow hard upon that opening section have these titles: "The Void Cantos," "Death and Death's Mirror," and "The Dark Corridor to Heaven." These are very dark poems indeed, and very inventive in their celebration of darkness and the macabre. The foreword by John Foster and the preface by Sheppard himself can serve as an erudite and more than adequate guide to the poet's creativity and mentality much more than anything that we could write. As expressed on the back cover, this volume does in fact announce "a cold poetics of the macabre in the new dark age of the Anthropocene," emphasis on that *po,* if not Poe himself. We shall restrict ourselves to quoting only two short pieces. In them, as in all the rest of the contents, the poet offers much to study and to engage us.

Nocturne No. 2

Night was my vigil; I sat it alone,
A nighttime of years never-ending,
Years by myself where light was unknown,
The darkness severe and unbending.
I came upon means in my decades-long fight
To only but briefly relive it,
And in certain moments I thought I'd found delight
But I was a fool to believe it.

Nocturne No. 4

A beauty in the darkness lies
For those that go with open heart;
And shadows cannot blind those eyes
For whom the darkness is a part.
Like roses grown on gravestones while
Illuminated in the gloom.
The dark is home to nighttime's child
And midnight is her constant groom.

But these brief pieces can only hint at the dark wealth of mood and imagination created and harvested here. Sheppard is an impeccable craftsman throughout the volume, no less than in the many longer poems cunningly distributed almost everywhere. The illustrations complement the selections to a T—that is, to perfection, even if we found them at times a distraction from the text itself. This is a handsome production, beautifully printed, and often of great variety and size in terms of typeface. However dark in theme, the collection is not repugnant, but it does just skirt the edge of repulsiveness. It does announce a new major voice in the genre of macabre poetry.

Notes on Contributors

Manuel Arenas is a writer of verse and prose in the Gothic Horror tradition. His work has appeared in various anthologies and journals including *Spectral Realms* and *Penumbra*. He currently resides in Phoenix, Arizona, where he pens his dark ditties sheltered behind heavy curtains, as he shuns the oppressive orb which glares down on him from the cloudless, dust-filled sky.

Chelsea Arrington has a predilection for things dark and romantic. Among her favorite authors are Algernon Charles Swinburne, Lord Dunsany, and Ray Bradbury. She likes her steaks rare and her wine as dry as graveyard dirt. Her poetry has appeared in the anthology *Folk Horror Revival: Corpse Roads*, *Spectral Realms*, and *The Audient Void*. She lives in Southern California with her boyfriend, her nephew, and two lap dogs.

David Barker is coauthor of three books of Lovecraftian fiction with the late W. H. Pugmire: *The Revenant of Rebecca Pascal*, *In the Gulfs of Dream and Other Lovecraftian Tales*, and *Witches in Dreamland*. His collection of horror fiction, *Her Wan Embrace*, is due from Weird House Press in 2021, and he has a story in *A Walk in a Darker Wood: An Anthology of Folk Horror* (Oxygen Man Books, 2020).

Leigh Blackmore's horror fiction has appeared in over sixty magazines from *Avatar* to *Strange Detective Stories*. He has reviewed for journals including *Lovecraft Annual*, *Shoggoth*, *Skinned Alive*, and *Dead Reckonings*. His critical essays appear in volumes including Benjamin Szumskyj's *The Man Who Collected Psychos: Critical Essays on Robert Bloch*, Gary William Crawford's *Ramsey Campbell: Critical Essays on the Modern Master of Horror*, Danel Olson's *21st Century Gothic*, and elsewhere. New weird verse appears or is forthcoming in *Penumbra* and other journals.

Adam Bolivar, a native of Boston now residing in Portland, Oregon, has published his weird fiction and poetry in the pages of *Nameless*, the *Lovecraft eZine*, *Spectral Realms*, and Chaosium's *Steampunk Cthulhu* and *Atomic Age Cthulhu* anthologies. His latest collection, *The Lay of Old Hex*, was published in 2017 by Hippocampus Press.

G. O. Clark's writing has been published in *Asimov's*, *Analog*, *Space & Time*, *Midnight under the Big Top*, *Daily SF*, *HWA Poetry Showcase VII*, and many other publications over the last thirty years. He is the author of fifteen poetry collections, the most recent being *Easy Travel to the Stars* (2020). His second fiction collection, *Twist and Turns*, came out in 2016. He won the Asimov's Readers Award for poetry in 2001 and was Stoker Award finalist in 2011. He is retired, and lives in Davis, California.

Frank Coffman is a retired professor of college English, creative writing, and journalism. He has published speculative poetry, fiction, and scholarly essays in a variety of journals, magazines, and anthologies. His poetic magnum opus, *The Coven's Hornbook and Other Poems* (2019), has been followed by another large collection of speculative poetry, *Black Flames and Gleaming Shadows* (2020). Both books are available from Bold Venture Press and on Amazon.

Scott J. Couturier is a writer of the weird, grotesque, perverse, and darkly fantastic. His prose and poetry have appeared in numerous venues, including *The Audient Void*, *Spectral Realms*, *Hinnom Magazine*, *Eternal Haunted Summer*, *Weirdbook*, and the *Test Patterns & Pulps* series of anthologies from Planet X Publications. He lives an elusive reverie in the wilds of Northern Michigan.

Harris Coverley was long-listed for the 2020 Rhysling Award, Short Poems category, and is a member of the Weird Poets Society. He has verse most recently appearing in *Star*Line*, *Scifaikuest*, *The Oddville Press*, *Yellow Mama*, and *View from Atlantis*, among many others, along with short fiction in *Curiosities*, *Hypnos*, and *Eldritch Journal*. He lives in Manchester, England.

Ashley Dioses is a writer of dark fantasy and horror poetry from Southern California. Her debut poetry collection, *Diary of a Sorceress*, was released from Hippocampus Press in 2017. Her second collection of early works, *The Withering*, appeared from Jackanapes Press in 2020. Her poem "Cobwebs" is mentioned in Ellen Datlow's *Best Horror of the Year, Volume Twelve*. She was also a nominee for the 2019 Pushcart Prize. She is currently an active member in the HWA and a member of the SFPA.

Ian Futter began writing stories and poems in his childhood, but only lately has started to share them. One of his poems appears in *The Darke Phantastique* (Cycatrix Press, 2014), and he continues to produce dark fiction for admirers of the surreal.

Wade German is the author of the poetry collections *Dreams from a Black Nebula*, *The Ladies of the Everlasting Lichen and Other Relics*, and *Incantations*, a selection of his verse in Portuguese translation that was also released as a digital audio album. His latest book is the verse drama *Children of Hypnos*.

Thomas Goff feels Clark Ashton Smith's uncanny presence whenever he travels to Auburn, California, to play trumpet with the Auburn Symphony. Tom is represented in *Fire and Rain: Ecopoetry of California* (Scarlet Tanager Press, 2018) and in *Twelve-Tone Row: Music in Words* (I Street Press, 2018), his first full-length poetry collection.

Maxwell I. Gold is a Rhysling Award–nominated author of weird fiction, writing short stories and prose poems that center on his profane Cyber Gods Mythos. His work has appeared in numerous publications including *The Audient Void*, *Space and Time*, *Weirdbook*, and many others.

Clay F. Johnson is an amateur pianist with an unreasonable obsession for Gothic literature and Romantic-era poetry. His writing has been featured in the Horror Writers Association's *Poetry Showcase*, nominated for a Rhysling Award and Pushcart Prize, and received Honorable Mention in *The Best Horror of the Year*. His first collection of poetry, *A Ride through Faerie and Other Poems*, is forthcoming in 2021.

S. T. Joshi is a widely published critic and editor. He has prepared editions of the collected poetry of H. P. Lovecraft, Clark Ashton Smith,

Donald Wandrei, George Sterling, and H. L. Mencken. He is the editor of *Spectral Realms*.

David C. Kopaska-Merkel assumed human form in the 1950s. As a cover, he edited *Star*Line* in the late '90s and won the Rhysling award (long poem) in 2006 for "The Tin Men" (a collaboration with Kendall Evans). His poetry has been published in venues including *Asimov's*, *Strange Horizons*, *Polu Texni*, *Primate Cuisine,* and *Night Cry*. He has written 31 books and edits *Dreams and Nightmares* magazine.

Lori R. Lopez is a quirky author, illustrator, poet, and songwriter who likes to wear hats. Her poetry collection *Darkverse: The Shadow Hours* was nominated for the 2018 Elgin Award, and two poems have been nominated for the 2020 Rhysling Award. Other titles include *The Dark Mister Snark, Leery Lane,* and *An Ill Wind Blows*. Learn about her books at fairyflyentertainment.com, a website shared with two talented sons.

Charles Lovecraft studies English at Macquarie University, Sydney. His main literary and life influences have been H. P. Lovecraft and macabre literature. More than 150 of his poems have been published. As publisher-editor he runs weird poetry imprint P'rea Press (www.preapress.com). He is working on a long Lovecraftian weird poem, *The Caller of Darkness,* and has edited thirty-four books.

Josh Maybrook is an American poet living in Edinburgh, Scotland. His poems, written largely in traditional verse forms, draw influence from weird fiction, classical mythology, and long walks in rural landscapes.

Ngo Binh Anh Khoa is a teacher of English in Ho Chi Minh City, Vietnam. In his free time, he enjoys daydreaming, reading, and occasionally writing poetry for personal entertainment. His speculative poems have appeared in NewMyths.com, *Heroic Fantasy Quarterly, The Audient Void,* and other venues.

K. A. Opperman is a poet with a predilection for the strange, the Gothic, and the grotesque, continuing the macabre and fantastical tradition of such luminaries as Poe, Clark Ashton Smith, and H. P.

Lovecraft. His first verse collection, *The Crimson Tome*, was published by Hippocampus Press in 2015.

Manuel Pérez-Campos's poetry has appeared previously in *Spectral Realms* and *Weird Fiction Review*. A collection of his poetry in the key of the weird is in progress; so is a collection of ground-breaking essays on H. P. Lovecraft. He lives in Bayamón, Puerto Rico.

Carl E. Reed is currently employed as the showroom manager for a window, siding, and door company just outside Chicago. Former jobs include U.S. marine, long-haul trucker, improvisational actor, cab driver, security guard, bus driver, door-to-door encyclopedia salesman, construction worker, and art show MC. His poetry has been published in the *Iconoclast* and *Spectral Realms*; short stories in *Black Gate* and *newWitch* magazines.

Geoffrey Reiter is Associate Professor and Coordinator of Literature at Lancaster Bible College. He is also an Associate Editor at the website *Christ and Pop Culture*, where he frequently writes about weird horror and dark fantasy. As a scholar of weird fiction, Reiter has published academic articles on such authors as Arthur Machen, Bram Stoker, Clark Ashton Smith, and William Peter Blatty.

Allan Rozinski is a writer of speculative poetry and fiction. His poetry and fiction has most recently been accepted or published in *Spectral Realms*, *Weirdbook*, *Star*Line*, *The Literary Hatchet*, and *The 2020 Rhysling Anthology*. His 2020 Rhysling-nominated poems are "The Solace of the Father Moon" (short category) and "Cannibal Rex" (long category).

David Schembri is an author and genre poet from Australia. He is the author of *Unearthly Fables* (in collaboration with The Writing Show, 2013) and the Australian Shadows Awards–nominated collection *Beneath the Ferny Tree* (Close-Up Books, 2018). His poetry has appeared in several issues of *Spectral Realms* as well as in the *Anno Klarkash-Ton* anthology by Rainfall Books and issue 13 of Midnight Echo Magazine.

Ann K. Schwader lives and writes in Colorado. Her most recent collections are *Dark Energies* (P'rea Press, 2015) and *Twisted in Dream*

(Hippocampus Press, 2011). A new collection, *Unquiet Stars*, is forthcoming from Weird House. Her *Wild Hunt of the Stars* (Sam's Dot, 2010) and *Dark Energies* were Bram Stoker Award finalists. In 2018, she received the Science Fiction & Fantasy Poetry Association's Grand Master award. She is also a two-time Rhysling Award winner.

Darrell Schweitzer is a former editor of *Weird Tales* (1988–2007) and a widely published author of weird fiction. A two-volume retrospective of his best work, *The Mysteries of the Faceless King* and *The Last Heretic*, have recently appeared from PS Publishing. He is still overdue for another poetry collection.

Donald Sidney-Fryer is the author of *Emperor of Dreams: A Clark Ashton Smith Bibliography* (Donald M. Grant, 1978), *The Atlantis Fragments* (Hippocampus Press, 2009), and many other volumes. He has edited Smith's *Poems in Prose* (Arkham House, 1965) and written many books and articles on California poets. His autobiography *Hobgoblin Apollo* (2016) and two volumes of miscellany, *Aesthetics Ho!* (2017) and *West of Wherevermore* (2019), have been published by Hippocampus Press.

Claire Smith writes poetry about other worlds. Her work regularly appears in *Spectral Realms*. Most recently her poems have also featured in *Songs of Eretz, Corvid Queen, Illumen,* and *Sage Cigarettes*. She holds an M.A. in English from the Open University and is currently studying for a Ph.D. at the University of Gloucestershire. Claire lives in Gloucestershire with her husband and their very spoiled Tonkinese cat, Ishtar.

Oliver Smith is a visual artist and writer from Cheltenham, UK. His poetry has appeared in *Mirror Dance, Dreams & Nightmares, Rivet, Strange Horizons, Liminality,* and *Penumbric*. Oliver was awarded first place in the BSFS 2019 competition for his poem "Better Living through Witchcraft," and his poem "Lost Palace, Lighted Tracks" was nominated for the 2020 Pushcart Prize. In 2020 he was awarded a Ph.D. in Literary and Critical Studies.

Christina Sng is the Bram Stoker Award–winning author of *A Collection of Nightmares*, Elgin Award runner-up *Astropoetry*, and *A Collection of*

Dreamscapes. Her poetry, fiction, and art have been published in numerous venues worldwide, and her work has garnered nominations in the Rhysling Awards, the Dwarf Stars, and the Elgin Awards, as well as honorable mentions in *The Year's Best Fantasy and Horror* and *The Best Horror of the Year*. Christina's first novelette, *Fury*, appears in *Black Cranes: Tales of Unquiet Women*, and her next poetry collection, *The Gravity of Existence*, is forthcoming in 2022.

DJ Tyrer is the person behind Atlantean Publishing and has been published in *The Rhysling Anthology 2016*, issues of *Cyäegha*, *The Horrorzine*, *Scifaikuest*, *Sirens Call*, *Star*Line*, *Tigershark*, and *The Yellow Zine*. The echapbook *One Vision* is available from Tigershark Publishing. *SuperTrump* and *A Wuhan Whodunnit* are available for download from Atlantean Publishing.

Steven Withrow's most recent verse collection is *The Bedlam Philharmonic*. His poems appear in *Spectral Realms*, *Asimov's Science Fiction*, and *Dreams & Nightmares*. His short poem "The Sun Ships," from a collection of the same title, was nominated for a 2016 Rhysling Award from the Science Fiction & Fantasy Poetry Association. He lives in Falmouth, Massachusetts.

Jordan Zuniga is an emerging poet, aspiring author, and an avid gamer. He regularly writes prose and poetry on Instagram. He is eagerly seeking opportunity to share his work.

CPSIA information can be obtained
at www.ICGtesting.com
Printed in the USA
BVHW041357150321
602477BV00004B/21